A Warrior's Mindset

The Training Guide to Develop a Mindset for Greatness

By Michael Adams

A Warrior's Mindset

The Training Guide to Develop a Mindset for Greatness

By Michael Adams

Printed by CreateSpaceCreated and published through the Influence to Publishing Profits Training Quote Book Generator

Printed in the United States of America 10 9 8 7 6 5 4 3 2

Introduction

Greatness is simply the part of you that wants more, the desire you hold to be more. It operates in you for a purpose. It calls you from the inside, like a whisper constantly nudging you to expand and step out of your zone of comfort. If your like most people, you stay stuck in fear because this is what you've always known. Imagine you continue to stay in this place of fear never doing what you desire to do and feeling the regret of never making progress. What will your life look like one year from now, if you remain fearful? Now compound that over five years. Ten years.

For most people who are at the end of their life and asked the question, "What were some of the best memories in your life?" They began to share all the things they never completed and all the things they WISH they did. So, I ask you the question, "What will you be saying at the end of your life?" Remember, there is no guarantee of tomorrow, next week, or next year. Life is happening right now, as you read these words.

A Warrior's Mindset is a training guide for developing a mindset for your inner greatness. You are alive right now because there is a life force that is in you and all expansive. This part of you is the inner warrior that walks with great love, pride, courage, humility, care and strength. It is the part of you that seeks greater things in life, the part of you that calls you to step beyond. Imagine how much greater your life can be when you step into this warrior and live as you want to live. Imagine the things that will open up for you. Imagine what becomes possible when you align yourself with that warrior.

The voice of doubt that keeps you in fear is only a result of your PAST circumstances. Just think, all the experiences that have happened in the PAST have constructed this voice of doubt. If you are living in fear, it's because things haven't gone your way in the PAST. Just think, how much of our present where ANYTHING IS POSSIBLE is affected by our evidence of the past. What will happen or not happen in your life if this voice of doubt that is just your story of all the things that didn't go your way, continues to control your life?

This book is designed to bring you back into the POSSIBLE. Repetition is the mother of all learning, so start now to develop your mindset to unleash your inner warrior. Let's begin...

Instructions to develop the Warrior:

1. Read Quote once a day.

2. Answer questions after reflecting on quote.

3. Close your eyes and sit for 10 minutes seeing, hearing, and feeling the thing you desire as you already have it now. Your mind does not know the difference between real and imagined, so the more you can create the vivid imagery, the more your mind will attract to it.

4. Look for evidence that what you desire is coming to you now.

5. How you FEEL will bring you what you FEEL, so work on FEELING happy, love, abundance, well-being, etc.

I challenge you to do these tasks daily and you will see the power of your mind. You are simply retraining your mind to attract what you want. The Law of Attraction is always at work, just like the Law of Gravity. Whether you believe it or not, it is bringing you the thoughts and feelings you most focus on.

"The first step towards getting somewhere is to decide that you are not going to stay where you are." – J. P. Morgan

Look at your current performance in life. What are you unsatisfied with? What do you dislike about your position now? Can you do better? If yes, make a decision that from this moment you will do everything in your power to achieve the greatness that lies before you.

Questions to develop the Warrior within:
My mind will always give me more of what I focus on. Therefore, I am grateful for…

_____

_____

_____

What do I need to hear today to keep expanding and moving forward?

_____

_____

_____

What are 3 things I can complete to make today a success?

_____

_____

_____

What pictures am I creating right now about that future I want?

_____

_____

_____

The mind does not know the difference between real and imagined, so see yourself already having your desires right now and watch it become reality. Close your eyes and see, hear, touch, and feel it.

"Set Your Course Captain! You are the Captain of your ship! A ship without a destination will always go no where." -Michael Adams

As the captain, you must make a decision. A decision means coming to a conclusion after consideration. So, come to a conclusion in your mind on what you want. You deserve the best, so set your destination for something big. How big will you dream?

Questions to develop the Warrior within:
My mind will always give me more of what I focus on. Therefore, I am grateful for…

_____

_____

_____

What do I need to hear today to keep expanding and moving forward?

_____

_____

_____

What are 3 things I can complete to make today a success?

_____

_____

_____

What pictures am I creating right now about that future I want?

_____

_____

_____

The mind does not know the difference between real and imagined, so see yourself already having your desires right now and watch it become reality. Close your eyes and see, hear, touch, and feel it.

"The Separation is in the Preparation" - Russell Wilson

Preparation: the actions or things we do to get ready for an undertaking. How you do anything is how you do everything. Would someone see you preparing for success or preparing to fail? Remember we want to always be creating separation from the person we are today. Develop, Grow, Expand. That means getting better daily. You Got This!

Questions to develop the Warrior within:
My mind will always give me more of what I focus on. Therefore, I am grateful for…

_____

_____

_____

What do I need to hear today to keep expanding and moving forward?

_____

_____

What are 3 things I can complete to make today a success?

_____

_____

_____

What pictures am I creating right now about that future I want?

_____

_____

_____

The mind does not know the difference between real and imagined, so see yourself already having your desires right now and watch it become reality. Close your eyes and see, hear, touch, and feel it.

"Sometimes when you are in a dark place, you think you've been buried, but you've actually been planted. - The Unbounded Spirit

Retrain your mind to reframe your thinking so you are expanding, not contracting. Look for 7 different ways you can interpret any given situation. Choose the way that makes you feel strongest. If you can't see it, ask someone else.

Questions to develop the Warrior within:
My mind will always give me more of what I focus on. Therefore, I am grateful for...

_____

_____

_____

What do I need to hear today to keep expanding and moving forward?

_____

_____

_____

What are 3 things I can complete to make today a success?

_____

_____

_____

What pictures am I creating right now about that future I want?

_____

_____

_____

The mind does not know the difference between real and imagined, so see yourself already having your desires right now and watch it become reality. Close your eyes and see, hear, touch, and feel it.

"Potential is your Greatest Treasure and Super Power. It is buried deep beneath Fear, Frustration, and Anger. Do you dare to dig? - Michael Adams

What if there was something hidden within you, a superpower, and the only way to acquire it was to move outside your zone of comfort. Are your taking actions to explore beyond your fear? Are you moving past the frustration you experience when something is difficult or hard?

Questions to develop the Warrior within:
My mind will always give me more of what I focus on. Therefore, I am grateful for…

_____

_____

_____

What do I need to hear today to keep expanding and moving forward?

_____

_____

_____

What are 3 things I can complete to make today a success?

_____

_____

_____

What pictures am I creating right now about that future I want?

_____

_____

_____

The mind does not know the difference between real and imagined, so see yourself already having your desires right now and watch it become reality. Close your eyes and see, hear, touch, and feel it.

"Life is 10% what happens to you and 90% how you react to it. -Charles R. Swindoll

Imagine that, 90% of your life is in your control. 10% will be unexpected surprises that will challenge and test you. Ask yourself, what do I do when I am faced with an obstacle? Is what I do now holding me back or moving me forward? What reactions do I need to work on? Ask someone for feedback.

Questions to develop the Warrior within:
My mind will always give me more of what I focus on. Therefore, I am grateful for...

_____

_____

_____

What do I need to hear today to keep expanding and moving forward?

_____

_____

_____

What are 3 things I can complete to make today a success?

_____

_____

_____

What pictures am I creating right now about that future I want?

_____

_____

_____

The mind does not know the difference between real and imagined, so see yourself already having your desires right now and watch it become reality. Close your eyes and see, hear, touch, and feel it.

"Excuses are the nails used to build the house of failure. -Unknown

Excuse: a reason or explanation put forward to defend a fault or lack of result. We all know how to make excuses, some are just better at it than others. Let them continue to build mansions of failure. Remove your excuses, own your faults and results, then your life will be everything you have dreamed.

Questions to develop the Warrior within:
My mind will always give me more of what I focus on. Therefore, I am grateful for...

_____

_____

_____

What do I need to hear today to keep expanding and moving forward?

_____

_____

_____

What are 3 things I can complete to make today a success?

_____

_____

_____

What pictures am I creating right now about that future I want?

_____

_____

_____

The mind does not know the difference between real and imagined, so see yourself already having your desires right now and watch it become reality. Close your eyes and see, hear, touch, and feel it.

"A bad attitude is like a flat tire, you can't go anywhere until you change it. -Unknown

When you feel you are making no progress in life and things are not going the way you want, look at your attitude. Remember a bad attitude is a negative way of thinking or feeling about someone or something. Negativity will keep your tire flat and unable to move, fix it now! Ask yourself what is another way I can look at this?

Questions to develop the Warrior within:
My mind will always give me more of what I focus on. Therefore, I am grateful for...

_____

_____

_____

What do I need to hear today to keep expanding and moving forward?

_____

_____

_____

What are 3 things I can complete to make today a success?

_____

_____

_____

What pictures am I creating right now about that future I want?

_____

_____

_____

The mind does not know the difference between real and imagined, so see yourself already having your desires right now and watch it become reality. Close your eyes and see, hear, touch, and feel it.

"You will receive a body. You may love it or hate it, but its yours for the entire time you're here, so accept it. -Cherie Carter-Scott

The body you were gifted was hand picked just for you. The sooner you accept everything about your body, the quicker you can put it to work. Your body is your vehicle, so put in the destination. Treat your body as a $1,000,000 mansion that you get to call home.

Questions to develop the Warrior within:
My mind will always give me more of what I focus on. Therefore, I am grateful for…

_____

_____

_____

What do I need to hear today to keep expanding and moving forward?

_____

_____

_____

What are 3 things I can complete to make today a success?

_____

_____

_____

What pictures am I creating right now about that future I want?

_____

_____

_____

The mind does not know the difference between real and imagined, so see yourself already having your desires right now and watch it become reality. Close your eyes and see, hear, touch, and feel it.

"You are the average of the 5 people you spend the most time with. -Jim Rohn

After conducting multiple studies, researchers found that a person's top 5 friends that they spent the most time with were numerically similar on multiple levels including financial, relational, spiritual, etc. If you desire more in your life, how might the people you surround yourself around daily be affecting your outcomes and performance?

Questions to develop the Warrior within:
My mind will always give me more of what I focus on. Therefore, I am grateful for…

_____

_____

_____

What do I need to hear today to keep expanding and moving forward?

_____

_____

_____

What are 3 things I can complete to make today a success?

_____

_____

_____

What pictures am I creating right now about that future I want?

_____

_____

_____

The mind does not know the difference between real and imagined, so see yourself already having your desires right now and watch it become reality. Close your eyes and see, hear, touch, and feel it.

"When we are no longer able to change a situation... we are challenged to change ourselves. -Viktor E. Frankl

Your desire to change a situation is directly related to your expectation of the outcome. What situation have you been trying to change in your life? What have been the results of your efforts? Maybe its time, you look at yourself and ask how can I approach this differently? What can I improve about myself? When you change, your life can change.

Questions to develop the Warrior within:
My mind will always give me more of what I focus on. Therefore, I am grateful for...

_____

_____

_____

What do I need to hear today to keep expanding and moving forward?

_____

_____

_____

What are 3 things I can complete to make today a success?

_____

_____

_____

What pictures am I creating right now about that future I want?

_____

_____

_____

The mind does not know the difference between real and imagined, so see yourself already having your desires right now and watch it become reality. Close your eyes and see, hear, touch, and feel it.

"Others are merely mirrors of you. You cannot love or hate something about another person unless it reflects to you something you love or hate about yourself. - Cherie Carter-Scott

You have to know how something looks to be able to recognize it. Therefore, know that everything you can see in others is just your mind bringing attention to some things you may need to heal in yourself. See beauty, get beauty.

Questions to develop the Warrior within:
My mind will always give me more of what I focus on. Therefore, I am grateful for…

_____

_____

_____

What do I need to hear today to keep expanding and moving forward?

_____

_____

_____

What are 3 things I can complete to make today a success?

_____

_____

_____

What pictures am I creating right now about that future I want?

_____

_____

_____

The mind does not know the difference between real and imagined, so see yourself already having your desires right now and watch it become reality. Close your eyes and see, hear, touch, and feel it.

"Strength doesn't come from what you can do, it comes from overcoming the things you once thought you couldn't. -Rikki Rogers

Imagine that time in your life when you thought you couldn't do something. Now recognize how you overcame that one thing. You beliefs changed as a result of you doing it. Realize all the strength you have already developed. Now make it a game and see how many more things you can overcome.

Questions to develop the Warrior within:
My mind will always give me more of what I focus on. Therefore, I am grateful for...

_____

_____

_____

What do I need to hear today to keep expanding and moving forward?

_____

_____

What are 3 things I can complete to make today a success?

_____

_____

_____

What pictures am I creating right now about that future I want?

_____

_____

_____

The mind does not know the difference between real and imagined, so see yourself already having your desires right now and watch it become reality. Close your eyes and see, hear, touch, and feel it.

"Expectation placed on people is called disappointment, Expectation placed on a goal is called Progress. -Michael Adams

Expectation is a strong belief that something will happen. Placing expectation on other people is almost guaranteed to lead you toward disappointment. Allow others to just be, if you can accept this relational problems simply melt away to nothing.

Questions to develop the Warrior within:
My mind will always give me more of what I focus on. Therefore, I am grateful for…

_____

_____

_____

What do I need to hear today to keep expanding and moving forward?

_____

_____

_____

What are 3 things I can complete to make today a success?

_____

_____

_____

What pictures am I creating right now about that future I want?

_____

_____

_____

The mind does not know the difference between real and imagined, so see yourself already having your desires right now and watch it become reality. Close your eyes and see, hear, touch, and feel it.

"The starting point of all achievement is desire. - Napolean Hill

Do you have desire? Desire is a strong intense feeling of wanting to have something or wishing to have something happen. Truth is, we have all acted on our desires in one point in our lives. Now ask yourself, what do I want? Now, build that desire! What would make you want it even more?

Questions to develop the Warrior within:
My mind will always give me more of what I focus on. Therefore, I am grateful for...

_____

_____

_____

What do I need to hear today to keep expanding and moving forward?

_____

_____

_____

What are 3 things I can complete to make today a success?

_____

_____

_____

What pictures am I creating right now about that future I want?

_____

_____

_____

The mind does not know the difference between real and imagined, so see yourself already having your desires right now and watch it become reality. Close your eyes and see, hear, touch, and feel it.

"Greet each morning with appreciation and thanks. Just because we don't see our blessings right then, we are always surrounded with them! - Marissa Adams

If you can actively greet each morning with an attitude of gratitude, you will shift the way you see your day. You will admire your body's amazing ability to breathe and notice all the luxuries that you have in your life.

Questions to develop the Warrior within:
My mind will always give me more of what I focus on. Therefore, I am grateful for...

_____

_____

_____

What do I need to hear today to keep expanding and moving forward?

_____

_____

_____

What are 3 things I can complete to make today a success?

_____

_____

_____

What pictures am I creating right now about that future I want?

_____

_____

_____

The mind does not know the difference between real and imagined, so see yourself already having your desires right now and watch it become reality. Close your eyes and see, hear, touch, and feel it.

"How you make others feel about themselves, says a lot about you. -Gratitude Habitat

What are your actions saying about you? Good or Bad? Remember, you rise when you lift others. How are you being friendly, generous, and considerate today? Are you looking to rise above or join the crowd down below? Choice is always yours.

Questions to develop the Warrior within:
My mind will always give me more of what I focus on. Therefore, I am grateful for…

_____

_____

_____

What do I need to hear today to keep expanding and moving forward?

_____

_____

_____

What are 3 things I can complete to make today a success?

_____

_____

_____

What pictures am I creating right now about that future I want?

_____

_____

_____

The mind does not know the difference between real and imagined, so see yourself already having your desires right now and watch it become reality. Close your eyes and see, hear, touch, and feel it.

"Gratitude is an art of painting an adversity into a lovely picture. -Kak Sri

Gratitude is the quality of being thankful, readiness to show appreciation for. Can you see the things in your life to be thankful for? Fact, You cannot feel sad and thankful at the same time. Sadness is focusing on what you don't have, while gratitude is focusing on and appreciating what you do have. Can you shift your focus?

Questions to develop the Warrior within:
My mind will always give me more of what I focus on. Therefore, I am grateful for...

_____

_____

What do I need to hear today to keep expanding and moving forward?

_____

_____

What are 3 things I can complete to make today a success?

_____

_____

What pictures am I creating right now about that future I want?

_____

_____

The mind does not know the difference between real and imagined, so see yourself already having your desires right now and watch it become reality. Close your eyes and see, hear, touch, and feel it.

"Dreams don't work unless you do. -John C. Maxwell

A Dream is a condition or achievement that is longed for, an aspiration. The ability to dream was GIFTED to you for a reason. Dreams represent the paradise you see in the distance, reality is where you are standing now. Work is the effort required to bring you closer to that paradise. What steps are you taking? Have you drawn out your steps? Just take that first step.

Questions to develop the Warrior within:
My mind will always give me more of what I focus on. Therefore, I am grateful for…

_____

_____

_____

What do I need to hear today to keep expanding and moving forward?

_____

_____

_____

What are 3 things I can complete to make today a success?

_____

_____

_____

What pictures am I creating right now about that future I want?

_____

_____

_____

The mind does not know the difference between real and imagined, so see yourself already having your desires right now and watch it become reality. Close your eyes and see, hear, touch, and feel it.

"If you do what you've always done, you'll get what you've always gotten. -Tony Robbins

Think about all your habits. You are simply the result of all your actions. If you don't have the grades you want, if you are a bad reader, if you don't have the relationship you want, then take different actions. We stay stuck, when we don't get curious enough to explore what's new and take the action to see the result.

Questions to develop the Warrior within:
My mind will always give me more of what I focus on. Therefore, I am grateful for…

_____

_____

_____

What do I need to hear today to keep expanding and moving forward?

_____

_____

_____

What are 3 things I can complete to make today a success?

_____

_____

_____

What pictures am I creating right now about that future I want?

_____

_____

_____

The mind does not know the difference between real and imagined, so see yourself already having your desires right now and watch it become reality. Close your eyes and see, hear, touch, and feel it.

"What good are our wings, without the courage to fly? -Atticus

Courage is displaying mental or moral strength to venture, persevere, and withstand danger, fear, or difficulty. Know that you have wings and you are meant to fly high in your life. Are you using your courage? You demonstrate courage in your life every time you tell yourself to Just Do It! Be Courageous!

Questions to develop the Warrior within:
My mind will always give me more of what I focus on. Therefore, I am grateful for...

_____

_____

_____

What do I need to hear today to keep expanding and moving forward?

_____

_____

What are 3 things I can complete to make today a success?

_____

_____

What pictures am I creating right now about that future I want?

_____

_____

The mind does not know the difference between real and imagined, so see yourself already having your desires right now and watch it become reality. Close your eyes and see, hear, touch, and feel it.

"Don't wait for the perfect moment, take the moment and make it perfect. -Zoey Sayward

You are in control of all the moments in your life. There are no perfect moments except for the ones you made possible. Many will say they are waiting for the perfect time, you will say okay enjoy the waiting. Every second, you have the power to control what you speak and what you do to make it your moment."

Questions to develop the Warrior within:
My mind will always give me more of what I focus on. Therefore, I am grateful for…

_____

_____

_____

What do I need to hear today to keep expanding and moving forward?

_____

_____

What are 3 things I can complete to make today a success?

_____

_____

_____

What pictures am I creating right now about that future I want?

_____

_____

_____

The mind does not know the difference between real and imagined, so see yourself already having your desires right now and watch it become reality. Close your eyes and see, hear, touch, and feel it.

"The fewer the facts, the stronger the opinion. -Arnold H. Glasow

You hear opinions everyday, which are views or judgments formed about someone or something, not necessarily based on fact or knowledge. Many people will allow others opinions to define their future. You see the problem with that? If someone just knew more of the story, they wouldn't have an opinion. They would present only facts.

Questions to develop the Warrior within:
My mind will always give me more of what I focus on. Therefore, I am grateful for…

_____

_____

_____

What do I need to hear today to keep expanding and moving forward?

_____

_____

What are 3 things I can complete to make today a success?

_____

_____

What pictures am I creating right now about that future I want?

_____

_____

_____

The mind does not know the difference between real and imagined, so see yourself already having your desires right now and watch it become reality. Close your eyes and see, hear, touch, and feel it.

"You can't start the next chapter of your life, if you keep re-reading your last one. -Unknown

Many will stay stuck in life, because they replay, rewind, replay, rewind negative memories in their mind. Remember we bring about what we think about. Seek the lesson or teaching from the past and move on, trust me your story gets better. Start creating a better story today.

Questions to develop the Warrior within:
My mind will always give me more of what I focus on. Therefore, I am grateful for…

_____

_____

_____

What do I need to hear today to keep expanding and moving forward?

_____

_____

_____

What are 3 things I can complete to make today a success?

_____

_____

_____

What pictures am I creating right now about that future I want?

_____

_____

_____

The mind does not know the difference between real and imagined, so see yourself already having your desires right now and watch it become reality. Close your eyes and see, hear, touch, and feel it.

"People are probably not happy with their lives, if their busy discussing yours. -Unknown

Gossip can be defined as reports about other people, typically involving details that are not confirmed as true. By passing false information, think about how that makes you look. We learn how to gossip, so we gossip. What you say about others casts a big bright light on you and the quality of your life.

Questions to develop the Warrior within:
My mind will always give me more of what I focus on. Therefore, I am grateful for…

_____

_____

_____

What do I need to hear today to keep expanding and moving forward?

_____

_____

_____

What are 3 things I can complete to make today a success?

_____

_____

_____

What pictures am I creating right now about that future I want?

_____

_____

_____

The mind does not know the difference between real and imagined, so see yourself already having your desires right now and watch it become reality. Close your eyes and see, hear, touch, and feel it.

"Whatever you hold in your mind on a consistent basis, is exactly what you will experience in your life. -Tony Robbins

Your mind is cooking whatever ingredients you are adding. Are you adding the ingredients that you want to create your most delicious, favorite meal? Pay attention to what you are allowing to enter your mind, for it will dictate your experience in life.

Questions to develop the Warrior within:
My mind will always give me more of what I focus on. Therefore, I am grateful for...

_____

_____

_____

What do I need to hear today to keep expanding and moving forward?

_____

_____

_____

What are 3 things I can complete to make today a success?

_____

_____

_____

What pictures am I creating right now about that future I want?

_____

_____

_____

The mind does not know the difference between real and imagined, so see yourself already having your desires right now and watch it become reality. Close your eyes and see, hear, touch, and feel it.

"Be helpful. When you see a person without a smile, give them yours. -Zig Ziglar

Even if we lost everything that was important to us, we still have the physical capacity to give a smile. How can you be helpful today? Are you spreading happiness and joy or keeping it to yourself? Remember you have a lot to give, so spread it around. You can't feel value without being valuable.

Questions to develop the Warrior within:
My mind will always give me more of what I focus on. Therefore, I am grateful for…

_____

_____

_____

What do I need to hear today to keep expanding and moving forward?

_____

_____

_____

What are 3 things I can complete to make today a success?

_____

_____

_____

What pictures am I creating right now about that future I want?

_____

_____

_____

The mind does not know the difference between real and imagined, so see yourself already having your desires right now and watch it become reality. Close your eyes and see, hear, touch, and feel it.

"Compassion is the process of building bridges to connect a gold heart to another. -Michael Adams

Compassion is having sorrow for another's misfortunes, while having a strong desire to alleviate the suffering. Demonstrating compassion requires one to view or experience another's misfortune, then take action to lessen the suffering. Seeing and knowing there is gold in others, will make you connect even more.

Questions to develop the Warrior within:
My mind will always give me more of what I focus on. Therefore, I am grateful for…

_____

_____

_____

What do I need to hear today to keep expanding and moving forward?

_____

_____

_____

What are 3 things I can complete to make today a success?

_____

_____

_____

What pictures am I creating right now about that future I want?

_____

_____

_____

The mind does not know the difference between real and imagined, so see yourself already having your desires right now and watch it become reality. Close your eyes and see, hear, touch, and feel it.

"Tell me and I forget. Teach me and I remember. Involve me and I learn. -Benjamin Franklin

How are you being in involved in your learning? Remember learning is the acquisition of knowledge or skills through experience or study. What knowledge and skills do you want to gain to carry with you on your journey? Ask yourself, how involved am I right now?

Questions to develop the Warrior within:
My mind will always give me more of what I focus on. Therefore, I am grateful for...

_____

_____

_____

What do I need to hear today to keep expanding and moving forward?

_____

_____

_____

What are 3 things I can complete to make today a success?

_____

_____

_____

What pictures am I creating right now about that future I want?

_____

_____

_____

The mind does not know the difference between real and imagined, so see yourself already having your desires right now and watch it become reality. Close your eyes and see, hear, touch, and feel it.

"Boredom: feeling weary because one is unoccupied or lacks interest in one's current activity.

Boredom is asking the question, What should I do? and immediately answering yourself with, There's nothing to do. Antidote to boredom: Curiousity. Ask yourself, what can I be curious about right now? If you say nothing, your amazing at being bored. Now become incredible at being CURIOUS.

Questions to develop the Warrior within:
My mind will always give me more of what I focus on. Therefore, I am grateful for...

_____

_____

_____

What do I need to hear today to keep expanding and moving forward?

_____

_____

_____

What are 3 things I can complete to make today a success?

_____

_____

_____

What pictures am I creating right now about that future I want?

_____

_____

_____

The mind does not know the difference between real and imagined, so see yourself already having your desires right now and watch it become reality. Close your eyes and see, hear, touch, and feel it.

"Service to others is the rent you pay, for your room here on earth. -Muhammad Ali

Service is the action of helping or doing work for someone. Are you paying your rent daily? There is much to be gained by being of service to others. Service is a verb, meaning it is something you do to help another. What acts of service can you do today or right now?

Questions to develop the Warrior within:
My mind will always give me more of what I focus on. Therefore, I am grateful for...

_____

_____

_____

What do I need to hear today to keep expanding and moving forward?

_____

_____

_____

What are 3 things I can complete to make today a success?

_____

_____

_____

What pictures am I creating right now about that future I want?

_____

_____

_____

The mind does not know the difference between real and imagined, so see yourself already having your desires right now and watch it become reality. Close your eyes and see, hear, touch, and feel it.

"The struggle you're in today is developing the strength you'll need for tomorrow. -Robert Tew

What if we could see our struggles today as mental exercise building the muscle strength needed for the larger challenges in the future? The truth is Problems never disappear, but as we get stronger problems turn into challenges. Ask your struggles, how can I increase my strength by overcoming this tough time?

Questions to develop the Warrior within:
My mind will always give me more of what I focus on. Therefore, I am grateful for...

_____

_____

_____

What do I need to hear today to keep expanding and moving forward?

_____

_____

_____

What are 3 things I can complete to make today a success?

_____

_____

_____

What pictures am I creating right now about that future I want?

_____

_____

_____

The mind does not know the difference between real and imagined, so see yourself already having your desires right now and watch it become reality. Close your eyes and see, hear, touch, and feel it.

"Be FEARLESS, and WATCH the world UNFOLD to your every DESIRE. -Kevin Abdulrahman

Fearless: LACK of an unpleasant emotion caused by the belief that someone or something is dangerous, likely to cause pain, or a threat. Fear is really the emotion that holds you back from your every desire. Learn to acknowledge your fear and DO IT ANYWAY!

Questions to develop the Warrior within:
My mind will always give me more of what I focus on. Therefore, I am grateful for...

_____

_____

_____

What do I need to hear today to keep expanding and moving forward?

_____

_____

_____

What are 3 things I can complete to make today a success?

_____

_____

_____

What pictures am I creating right now about that future I want?

_____

_____

_____

The mind does not know the difference between real and imagined, so see yourself already having your desires right now and watch it become reality. Close your eyes and see, hear, touch, and feel it.

"Responsibility is ACCEPTING that YOU are the CAUSE and the SOLUTION of the matter. - Anonymous

Responsibility: the state or fact of having a duty to deal with something. If every matter, you chose to be responsible to deal with something, you can see how you are now apart of the cause and solution. What can you gain from being at cause?

Questions to develop the Warrior within:
My mind will always give me more of what I focus on. Therefore, I am grateful for...

_____

_____

_____

What do I need to hear today to keep expanding and moving forward?

_____

_____

_____

What are 3 things I can complete to make today a success?

_____

_____

_____

What pictures am I creating right now about that future I want?

_____

_____

_____

The mind does not know the difference between real and imagined, so see yourself already having your desires right now and watch it become reality. Close your eyes and see, hear, touch, and feel it.

"Cultivation to the mind is as necessary as food to the body. -Marcus Cicero

Cultivation: the process of trying to develop a quality or skill. Imagine you are on a quest to develop your mind to a level of self-mastery because you know it will bear the greatest rewards for your life. All your dreams lie within the process of developing your mind. Seek to improve daily.

Questions to develop the Warrior within:
My mind will always give me more of what I focus on. Therefore, I am grateful for...

_____

_____

_____

What do I need to hear today to keep expanding and moving forward?

_____

_____

_____

What are 3 things I can complete to make today a success?

_____

_____

_____

What pictures am I creating right now about that future I want?

_____

_____

_____

The mind does not know the difference between real and imagined, so see yourself already having your desires right now and watch it become reality. Close your eyes and see, hear, touch, and feel it.

"The starting point of all achievement is DESIRE. Keep this constantly in mind. Weak desire brings weak results, just as a small fire makes a small amount of heat. -Napolean Hill

Remember desire is an intense, strong feeling of wanting to have something. Build your desire by turning up the intensity is why you must achieve your goals. The larger your fire, the harder it will be to put out.

Questions to develop the Warrior within:
My mind will always give me more of what I focus on. Therefore, I am grateful for...

_____

_____

_____

What do I need to hear today to keep expanding and moving forward?

_____

_____

_____

What are 3 things I can complete to make today a success?

_____

_____

_____

What pictures am I creating right now about that future I want?

_____

_____

_____

The mind does not know the difference between real and imagined, so see yourself already having your desires right now and watch it become reality. Close your eyes and see, hear, touch, and feel it.

"I'm on the hunt for who I've not yet become. - Unknown

Start your hunt if you have not started, there is an amazing fulfilling person stored inside you. On your hunting adventure is where you will eventually find him/her. The hunt is one of discovery, surprise, growth, and miracle. Find yourself by taking the first step into the unknown.

Questions to develop the Warrior within:
My mind will always give me more of what I focus on. Therefore, I am grateful for...

_____

_____

_____

What do I need to hear today to keep expanding and moving forward?

_____

_____

What are 3 things I can complete to make today a success?

_____

_____

What pictures am I creating right now about that future I want?

_____

_____

The mind does not know the difference between real and imagined, so see yourself already having your desires right now and watch it become reality. Close your eyes and see, hear, touch, and feel it.

"Everything we hear is an opinion, not a fact. Everything we see is perspective not the truth. -Marcus Aurelis

If opinions are just views or judgments formed individually about something or someone based on your perspective, can we ever know everything there is to know about that one thing? Can we ever see every angle of an event? No. So, stop the fight about wrong and right, it is a battle with no end.

Questions to develop the Warrior within:
My mind will always give me more of what I focus on. Therefore, I am grateful for...

_____

_____

_____

What do I need to hear today to keep expanding and moving forward?

_____

_____

_____

What are 3 things I can complete to make today a success?

_____

_____

_____

What pictures am I creating right now about that future I want?

_____

_____

_____

The mind does not know the difference between real and imagined, so see yourself already having your desires right now and watch it become reality. Close your eyes and see, hear, touch, and feel it.

"Hope is being able to see that there is light, despite all the darkness. -Desmond Tutu

In the darkest moments in life, we must keep our focus on the light. See that there is always new light in tomorrow, when the darkness appears overwhelming today. Inside your Hope, you will find a feeling of expectation and desire for a certain thing to happen. Keep your hope alive, by feeding it daily.

Questions to develop the Warrior within:
My mind will always give me more of what I focus on. Therefore, I am grateful for…

_____

_____

_____

What do I need to hear today to keep expanding and moving forward?

_____

_____

_____

What are 3 things I can complete to make today a success?

_____

_____

_____

What pictures am I creating right now about that future I want?

_____

_____

_____

The mind does not know the difference between real and imagined, so see yourself already having your desires right now and watch it become reality. Close your eyes and see, hear, touch, and feel it.

"Always find a reason to laugh. It may not add years to your life, but will certainly add life to your years. - Unknown

Find your reasons daily to express your laughter. In those moments, you are at peace with a joyful soul. Who are the people in your life that can make you laugh? What are things that make you laugh? Laughter is your body singing with amusement.

Questions to develop the Warrior within:
My mind will always give me more of what I focus on. Therefore, I am grateful for...

_____

_____

_____

What do I need to hear today to keep expanding and moving forward?

_____

_____

_____

What are 3 things I can complete to make today a success?

_____

_____

_____

What pictures am I creating right now about that future I want?

_____

_____

_____

The mind does not know the difference between real and imagined, so see yourself already having your desires right now and watch it become reality. Close your eyes and see, hear, touch, and feel it.

"Your mind will always believe everything you tell it. Feed it Hope. Feed it Truth. Feed it with Love. - Unknown

Your mind is a living breathing organism, if your paying attention, you get to choose what it eats. If you don't monitor your mind's eating habit, you will find it eating the bad, and therefore you will feel bad. Ask yourself, what do I need to feed my mind to get the best results I want?"

Questions to develop the Warrior within:
My mind will always give me more of what I focus on. Therefore, I am grateful for…

_____

_____

_____

What do I need to hear today to keep expanding and moving forward?

_____

_____

_____

What are 3 things I can complete to make today a success?

_____

_____

_____

What pictures am I creating right now about that future I want?

_____

_____

_____

The mind does not know the difference between real and imagined, so see yourself already having your desires right now and watch it become reality. Close your eyes and see, hear, touch, and feel it.

"There is something in this world you were put here to do that only you can do. -Unknown

Key word: Do. Do is an action. Your actions will lead you toward your purpose. Your purpose in life will be revealed to you when you take action to do things outside your zone of comfort. Go beyond yourself and open the fortune that lies in the growth. Like a seed's ability to expand, so is your ability.

Questions to develop the Warrior within:
My mind will always give me more of what I focus on. Therefore, I am grateful for…

_____

_____

_____

What do I need to hear today to keep expanding and moving forward?

_____

_____

_____

What are 3 things I can complete to make today a success?

_____

_____

_____

What pictures am I creating right now about that future I want?

_____

_____

_____

The mind does not know the difference between real and imagined, so see yourself already having your desires right now and watch it become reality. Close your eyes and see, hear, touch, and feel it.

"It is in your moments of decision that your DESTINY is shaped. -Tony Robbins

What is your destiny? What are you destined for? What do you want your destiny to be? Destiny may sound like something that is preplanned, but actually you are the driver who will determine your own Destiny in your moments of decision. You Decide What Your Destiny Will Be by your Decisions!"

Questions to develop the Warrior within:
My mind will always give me more of what I focus on. Therefore, I am grateful for...

_____

_____

_____

What do I need to hear today to keep expanding and moving forward?

_____

_____

What are 3 things I can complete to make today a success?

_____

_____

_____

What pictures am I creating right now about that future I want?

_____

_____

_____

The mind does not know the difference between real and imagined, so see yourself already having your desires right now and watch it become reality. Close your eyes and see, hear, touch, and feel it.

_____

"PATIENCE and FORTITUDE conquer all things. - Ralph Waldo Emerson

If you had the super power to create your best life, would you want it? Patience is the capacity to accept or tolerate delay, trouble, or suffering without getting angry or upset. Fortitude is the strength of mind that enables a person to encounter danger or bear pain or adversity with courage. Conquer now!

Questions to develop the Warrior within:
My mind will always give me more of what I focus on. Therefore, I am grateful for...

_____

_____

_____

What do I need to hear today to keep expanding and moving forward?

_____

_____

_____

What are 3 things I can complete to make today a success?

_____

_____

_____

What pictures am I creating right now about that future I want?

_____

_____

_____

The mind does not know the difference between real and imagined, so see yourself already having your desires right now and watch it become reality. Close your eyes and see, hear, touch, and feel it.

"Self confidence is the most attractive quality a person can have. How can anyone see how great you are if you can't see it yourself? -Unknown

Self confidence - a feeling of trust in one's abilities, qualities, and judgment. Now if there is low self-confidence that means the trust you have for yourself is not high. Trust is earned with small accomplishments that show you it's possible. Get those small wins and celebrate them!

Questions to develop the Warrior within:
My mind will always give me more of what I focus on. Therefore, I am grateful for…

_____

_____

_____

What do I need to hear today to keep expanding and moving forward?

_____

_____

_____

What are 3 things I can complete to make today a success?

_____

_____

_____

What pictures am I creating right now about that future I want?

_____

_____

_____

The mind does not know the difference between real and imagined, so see yourself already having your desires right now and watch it become reality. Close your eyes and see, hear, touch, and feel it.

"Don't wait until you have reached your goal to be proud of yourself. Be proud of every step you take toward that goal. -Unknown

To be proud is to feel a deep pleasure or satisfactions as a result of one's own achievements. Get into the habit of being proud for every action you take toward your goals or for each step you make to expand your comfort zone.

Questions to develop the Warrior within:
My mind will always give me more of what I focus on. Therefore, I am grateful for...

_____

_____

_____

What do I need to hear today to keep expanding and moving forward?

_____

_____

_____

What are 3 things I can complete to make today a success?

_____

_____

_____

What pictures am I creating right now about that future I want?

_____

_____

_____

The mind does not know the difference between real and imagined, so see yourself already having your desires right now and watch it become reality. Close your eyes and see, hear, touch, and feel it.

"Like the giant oak in the acorn seed, there too lies a giant within you. -Michael Adams

Just imagine for a moment that who you are today is no where close to the person you could be in the future. As life deals you the circumstances, know that it is only attempting to wake that sleeping giant within you.

LET IT AWAKE NOW!

Questions to develop the Warrior within:
My mind will always give me more of what I focus on. Therefore, I am grateful for…

_____

_____

_____

What do I need to hear today to keep expanding and moving forward?

_____

_____

_____

What are 3 things I can complete to make today a success?

_____

_____

_____

What pictures am I creating right now about that future I want?

_____

_____

_____

The mind does not know the difference between real and imagined, so see yourself already having your desires right now and watch it become reality. Close your eyes and see, hear, touch, and feel it.

"Abundance grows from the seed of every thank you. - Mary Davis

Abundance is bountifulness of the good things in life. Now you deserve all the good things in life. All the good things come from every seed of thank you's spoken. The more gratitude you can find in your life, the more love, happiness, joy, success, and achievement you will have in your life. The challenge is seeing your abundance.

Questions to develop the Warrior within:
My mind will always give me more of what I focus on. Therefore, I am grateful for...

_____

_____

_____

What do I need to hear today to keep expanding and moving forward?

_____

_____

_____

What are 3 things I can complete to make today a success?

_____

_____

_____

What pictures am I creating right now about that future I want?

_____

_____

_____

The mind does not know the difference between real and imagined, so see yourself already having your desires right now and watch it become reality. Close your eyes and see, hear, touch, and feel it.

"Whatever happens or doesn't happen in my life, I am to blame. -Michael Adams

What if you could say I take responsibility for everything that is good and not good in my life? There would be no room for blame towards anyone or anything else. This mindset shift requires you to be the central captain taking full blame if something doesn't turn out. Make sure you shift to lift!

Questions to develop the Warrior within:
My mind will always give me more of what I focus on. Therefore, I am grateful for...

_____

_____

_____

What do I need to hear today to keep expanding and moving forward?

_____

_____

What are 3 things I can complete to make today a success?

_____

_____

_____

What pictures am I creating right now about that future I want?

_____

_____

_____

The mind does not know the difference between real and imagined, so see yourself already having your desires right now and watch it become reality. Close your eyes and see, hear, touch, and feel it.

"Holding on to anger is like drinking poison and expecting the other person to die. -Buddha

Do you see the false expectation in this statement? When you are angry it is because you choose to believe someone has done you wrong. If anger is an arrow, there is always a target. We make the mistake of thinking the person to blame will be hit by our arrow. In the end, the arrow hits us and we hurt ourselves.

Questions to develop the Warrior within:
My mind will always give me more of what I focus on. Therefore, I am grateful for…

_____

_____

_____

What do I need to hear today to keep expanding and moving forward?

_____

_____

_____

What are 3 things I can complete to make today a success?

_____

_____

_____

What pictures am I creating right now about that future I want?

_____

_____

_____

The mind does not know the difference between real and imagined, so see yourself already having your desires right now and watch it become reality. Close your eyes and see, hear, touch, and feel it.

"Dwelling on the negative simply contributes to its power. -Shirley MacLaine

How much power are you giving to negativity? If you stop and think about it, negativity is typically a learned habit. It is a way of looking at events and choosing to see the negative aspects. Remember there is always a choice available. Negativity is just a choice that simply does nothing to improve your life.

Questions to develop the Warrior within:
My mind will always give me more of what I focus on. Therefore, I am grateful for...

_____

_____

_____

What do I need to hear today to keep expanding and moving forward?

_____

_____

_____

What are 3 things I can complete to make today a success?

_____

_____

_____

What pictures am I creating right now about that future I want?

_____

_____

_____

The mind does not know the difference between real and imagined, so see yourself already having your desires right now and watch it become reality. Close your eyes and see, hear, touch, and feel it.

"What you think... And what you Feel... And what Manifests is Always a Match, Every Single Time. No Exception. -Esther Hicks

Manifestation are the things that end up appearing or showing up. Therefore, you manifest the results in your life by your thoughts and feelings. The insight is, your thinking is directly linked to your feelings. And your thinking and feeling is linked to your reality.

Questions to develop the Warrior within:
My mind will always give me more of what I focus on. Therefore, I am grateful for...

_____

_____

_____

What do I need to hear today to keep expanding and moving forward?

_____

_____

_____

What are 3 things I can complete to make today a success?

_____

_____

_____

What pictures am I creating right now about that future I want?

_____

_____

_____

The mind does not know the difference between real and imagined, so see yourself already having your desires right now and watch it become reality. Close your eyes and see, hear, touch, and feel it.

"Speak things into existence. -Unknown

Never underestimate the enormous power within your words. You were blessed with the superpower of being able to Speak Things Into Existence. Every successful person will tell you all their success first started with the selection of their words. Now, what is it you'd like to bring into existence in your life? Can you observe your thinking and see the words you are using?

Questions to develop the Warrior within:
My mind will always give me more of what I focus on. Therefore, I am grateful for…

_____

_____

_____

What do I need to hear today to keep expanding and moving forward?

_____

_____

_____

What are 3 things I can complete to make today a success?

_____

_____

_____

What pictures am I creating right now about that future I want?

_____

_____

_____

The mind does not know the difference between real and imagined, so see yourself already having your desires right now and watch it become reality. Close your eyes and see, hear, touch, and feel it.

"You are what you do, not what you say you'll do. - Carl Jung

When it all comes down to it, the thing that will create separation from the person you are today to the person you want to be is ACTION. Action means the act or process of doing something to achieve an aim. Everyday you take actions, but are they actions toward what you want?

Questions to develop the Warrior within:
My mind will always give me more of what I focus on. Therefore, I am grateful for…

_____

_____

_____

What do I need to hear today to keep expanding and moving forward?

_____

_____

_____

What are 3 things I can complete to make today a success?

_____

_____

_____

What pictures am I creating right now about that future I want?

_____

_____

_____

The mind does not know the difference between real and imagined, so see yourself already having your desires right now and watch it become reality. Close your eyes and see, hear, touch, and feel it.

"Vision without Action is merely a Dream. Action without Vision simply passes the time. Vision with Action Can Change the World. -Joel A. Barker

How many amazing dreams will remain just a dream, with no action ever taken on them? How many people do we see just being busy, doing stuff with no vision or direction? Change the world by taking action on your life's vision!

Questions to develop the Warrior within:
My mind will always give me more of what I focus on. Therefore, I am grateful for…

_____

_____

_____

What do I need to hear today to keep expanding and moving forward?

_____

_____

_____

What are 3 things I can complete to make today a success?

_____

_____

_____

What pictures am I creating right now about that future I want?

_____

_____

_____

The mind does not know the difference between real and imagined, so see yourself already having your desires right now and watch it become reality. Close your eyes and see, hear, touch, and feel it.

"People learn how to treat you based on what you accept from them. -Unknown

Ask yourself, what am I allowing from others? What am I worth? Guaranteed that if you have a high self-worth, you will not take negative treatment from others. Low self-worth, you will stick around through all the ugliness. Where do you draw your boundaries in your life?

Questions to develop the Warrior within:
My mind will always give me more of what I focus on. Therefore, I am grateful for...

_____

_____

_____

What do I need to hear today to keep expanding and moving forward?

_____

_____

_____

What are 3 things I can complete to make today a success?

_____

_____

_____

What pictures am I creating right now about that future I want?

_____

_____

_____

The mind does not know the difference between real and imagined, so see yourself already having your desires right now and watch it become reality. Close your eyes and see, hear, touch, and feel it.

"If you keep blaming something or someone else for your problems, you will never learn why problems come your way. -Kushandwizdom.com

Many go through life thinking that others are the reason they have problems. Let me be your alarm clock. WAKE UP! You are responsible for everything that has happened to you. If you are the problem you are also the solution. Own It!

Questions to develop the Warrior within:
My mind will always give me more of what I focus on. Therefore, I am grateful for…

_____

_____

_____

What do I need to hear today to keep expanding and moving forward?

_____

_____

_____

What are 3 things I can complete to make today a success?

_____

_____

_____

What pictures am I creating right now about that future I want?

_____

_____

_____

The mind does not know the difference between real and imagined, so see yourself already having your desires right now and watch it become reality. Close your eyes and see, hear, touch, and feel it.

"The surest way to lose your self-worth is by trying to find it through the eyes of others. -Becca Lee

Self-worth means your own sense of value or worth. Imagine trying to find your worth or value by asking what others think, you would eventually be let down by what you find. Self-Worth is something only you can define! What are you worth? When did you decide that?

Questions to develop the Warrior within:
My mind will always give me more of what I focus on. Therefore, I am grateful for…

_____

_____

_____

What do I need to hear today to keep expanding and moving forward?

_____

_____

_____

What are 3 things I can complete to make today a success?

_____

_____

_____

What pictures am I creating right now about that future I want?

_____

_____

_____

The mind does not know the difference between real and imagined, so see yourself already having your desires right now and watch it become reality. Close your eyes and see, hear, touch, and feel it.

"Faith is like WiFi. It is invisible but it has the power to connect you to what you want. -GeniusQuotes

Faith is having a strong trust or confidence in someone or something. To have faith in yourself, is to have the utmost trust that you will make it. A person of strong faith will have no problem placing a $1,000,000 bet on themselves because they have a certainty in their own capacity.

Questions to develop the Warrior within:
My mind will always give me more of what I focus on. Therefore, I am grateful for…

_____

_____

_____

What do I need to hear today to keep expanding and moving forward?

_____

_____

_____

What are 3 things I can complete to make today a success?

_____

_____

_____

What pictures am I creating right now about that future I want?

_____

_____

_____

The mind does not know the difference between real and imagined, so see yourself already having your desires right now and watch it become reality. Close your eyes and see, hear, touch, and feel it.

"Your Golden key to happiness: Stand like a fountain and shower your appreciation every day in every way. - Michael Adams

It takes a series of gifts just to allow you life everyday. Your body, the air, water, this land, etc., are all available to you in abundant quantities. When you Fail to see all the gifts around you, you deny yourself happiness. See and appreciate all the gifts and life will give you even more!

Questions to develop the Warrior within:
My mind will always give me more of what I focus on. Therefore, I am grateful for…

_____

_____

_____

What do I need to hear today to keep expanding and moving forward?

_____

_____

_____

What are 3 things I can complete to make today a success?

_____

_____

_____

What pictures am I creating right now about that future I want?

_____

_____

_____

The mind does not know the difference between real and imagined, so see yourself already having your desires right now and watch it become reality. Close your eyes and see, hear, touch, and feel it.

"Sports do not build character, they reveal it. -John Wooden

Character can be seen by observing how a person thinks, feels and behaves. Character is more important than reputation, it is the way we handle ourselves when no one is looking. It is doing the right thing just because it is the right thing to do. How's your character? How do you act in privacy?

Questions to develop the Warrior within:
My mind will always give me more of what I focus on. Therefore, I am grateful for...

_____

_____

_____

What do I need to hear today to keep expanding and moving forward?

_____

_____

_____

What are 3 things I can complete to make today a success?

_____

_____

_____

What pictures am I creating right now about that future I want?

_____

_____

_____

The mind does not know the difference between real and imagined, so see yourself already having your desires right now and watch it become reality. Close your eyes and see, hear, touch, and feel it.

"I learned that courage was not the absence of fear, but the TRIUMPH over it. -Nelson Mandela

When doing something you fear, you know you are choosing the opposite which is COURAGE. Ask yourself right now, will I allow Fear or Courage to win? How long will you allow fear to be victorious in your mind? Now is the time to choose a new conqueror. Courage looks a whole lot better.

Questions to develop the Warrior within:
My mind will always give me more of what I focus on. Therefore, I am grateful for...

_____

_____

_____

What do I need to hear today to keep expanding and moving forward?

_____

_____

_____

What are 3 things I can complete to make today a success?

_____

_____

_____

What pictures am I creating right now about that future I want?

_____

_____

_____

The mind does not know the difference between real and imagined, so see yourself already having your desires right now and watch it become reality. Close your eyes and see, hear, touch, and feel it.

"The man who does more than he is paid for will soon be paid for more than he does. -Napolean Hill

It pays, literally, to put in the extra effort. Ask any person who has ever been moved up in life. The main reason they were moved up was not because of their experiences and qualifications, but their initiative to do more. By doing more they built up their karma points, now life just repaid them.

Questions to develop the Warrior within:
My mind will always give me more of what I focus on. Therefore, I am grateful for...

_____

_____

_____

What do I need to hear today to keep expanding and moving forward?

_____

_____

_____

What are 3 things I can complete to make today a success?

_____

_____

_____

What pictures am I creating right now about that future I want?

_____

_____

_____

The mind does not know the difference between real and imagined, so see yourself already having your desires right now and watch it become reality. Close your eyes and see, hear, touch, and feel it.

"Today I will do what other's won't, so tomorrow I can do what other's can't. -Unknown

If you want the privilege of doing the best jobs, you will do what everyone else around you is too scared to do. Taking the initiative to realizing your responsibility to make some things happen. Adding value by doing the actions others won't, speaks volumes! Another word used to describe this is "Initiative."

Questions to develop the Warrior within:
My mind will always give me more of what I focus on. Therefore, I am grateful for...

_____

_____

_____

What do I need to hear today to keep expanding and moving forward?

_____

_____

_____

What are 3 things I can complete to make today a success?

_____

_____

_____

What pictures am I creating right now about that future I want?

_____

_____

_____

The mind does not know the difference between real and imagined, so see yourself already having your desires right now and watch it become reality. Close your eyes and see, hear, touch, and feel it.

"Don't expect to see a change, if you don't make one. - John Assaraf

Sometimes we wonder why we can't get the results we want. The reason is because we fail to make a change to acquire the result. Change means to do something different than what you are used to. The world doesn't stay the same so why should you. Embrace change for it holds a new adventure.

Questions to develop the Warrior within:
My mind will always give me more of what I focus on. Therefore, I am grateful for...

_____

_____

_____

What do I need to hear today to keep expanding and moving forward?

_____

_____

_____

What are 3 things I can complete to make today a success?

_____

_____

_____

What pictures am I creating right now about that future I want?

_____

_____

_____

The mind does not know the difference between real and imagined, so see yourself already having your desires right now and watch it become reality. Close your eyes and see, hear, touch, and feel it.

"Failure is the opportunity to begin again more intelligently. -Henry Ford

Imagine the growth you could experience if your future failures could be seen in this light. You would welcome failures with excitement. Learn from the failures you experience and go after it again. That is the winner's equation for success. Failure is your opportunity to get better.

Questions to develop the Warrior within:
My mind will always give me more of what I focus on. Therefore, I am grateful for...

_____

_____

_____

What do I need to hear today to keep expanding and moving forward?

_____

_____

_____

What are 3 things I can complete to make today a success?

_____

_____

_____

What pictures am I creating right now about that future I want?

_____

_____

_____

The mind does not know the difference between real and imagined, so see yourself already having your desires right now and watch it become reality. Close your eyes and see, hear, touch, and feel it.

"If you change the way you look at things, the things you look at change. -Wayne Dyer

This is how you can change your environment around you completely. Infuse this mindset into your thinking. Mindset is a set of beliefs or a way of thinking that determines one's behavior, outlook and mental attitude. Change your mindset and change everything. It is all contained within.

Questions to develop the Warrior within:
My mind will always give me more of what I focus on. Therefore, I am grateful for...

_____

_____

_____

What do I need to hear today to keep expanding and moving forward?

_____

_____

What are 3 things I can complete to make today a success?

_____

_____

_____

What pictures am I creating right now about that future I want?

_____

_____

_____

The mind does not know the difference between real and imagined, so see yourself already having your desires right now and watch it become reality. Close your eyes and see, hear, touch, and feel it.

"If you want to succeed, double your failure rate. -Tom Watson

If you have the guts to embrace your fear and look it in the eye, make sure you meet up everyday. The more you can do to make fear your best friend, the more success you will acquire. Success hides behind the doors of fear. Open as many doors as you can. Failure is simply feedback to improve your performance.

Questions to develop the Warrior within:
My mind will always give me more of what I focus on. Therefore, I am grateful for…

_____

_____

_____

What do I need to hear today to keep expanding and moving forward?

_____

_____

_____

What are 3 things I can complete to make today a success?

_____

_____

_____

What pictures am I creating right now about that future I want?

_____

_____

_____

The mind does not know the difference between real and imagined, so see yourself already having your desires right now and watch it become reality. Close your eyes and see, hear, touch, and feel it.

"If you are not willing to learn, no one can help you. If you are determined to learn, no one can stop you. -Zig Ziglar

People can only be of help to you when you are willing to hear what they say. When you are determined to learn, you are saying "It is my right, I will acquire this information, I deserve the best... Watch out here I come." What are you determined to do?

Questions to develop the Warrior within:
My mind will always give me more of what I focus on. Therefore, I am grateful for…

_____

_____

_____

What do I need to hear today to keep expanding and moving forward?

_____

_____

_____

What are 3 things I can complete to make today a success?

_____

_____

_____

What pictures am I creating right now about that future I want?

_____

_____

_____

The mind does not know the difference between real and imagined, so see yourself already having your desires right now and watch it become reality. Close your eyes and see, hear, touch, and feel it.

"Whatever the mind can conceive and believe, the mind can achieve. -Napolean Hill

There are two ingredients that will carry you toward your dreams. First conceiving something means to have an idea or a dream. Second, believing means to accept that idea or dream as TRUTH, to be so sure of it happening. When these two forces combine, your mind is unlimited. Your only limit is that which you acknowledge.

Questions to develop the Warrior within:
My mind will always give me more of what I focus on. Therefore, I am grateful for...

_____

_____

_____

What do I need to hear today to keep expanding and moving forward?

_____

_____

What are 3 things I can complete to make today a success?

_____

_____

What pictures am I creating right now about that future I want?

_____

_____

_____

The mind does not know the difference between real and imagined, so see yourself already having your desires right now and watch it become reality. Close your eyes and see, hear, touch, and feel it.

"If you're bored with life, If you don't get up every morning with a burning desire to do things - You don't have enough goals. -Lou Holtz

Imagine, your boredom is only the result of not having enough goals. A Goal is the object of a person's ambition or effort, an aim or desired result. There are not enough targets in your life that you are shooting at. We stop setting goals when we experienced failure. Time To Reverse!

Questions to develop the Warrior within:
My mind will always give me more of what I focus on. Therefore, I am grateful for…

_____

_____

_____

What do I need to hear today to keep expanding and moving forward?

_____

_____

_____

What are 3 things I can complete to make today a success?

_____

_____

_____

What pictures am I creating right now about that future I want?

_____

_____

_____

The mind does not know the difference between real and imagined, so see yourself already having your desires right now and watch it become reality. Close your eyes and see, hear, touch, and feel it.

"Things turn out best for the people who make the best of the way things turn out. -John Wooden

Are you complaining about your situation? Are you spreading negativity? STOP! Look yourself in the mirror and say "I deserve more!" Now, make sure you are making the best out of your current circumstances. How can you change the way you are seeing things in your mind?

Questions to develop the Warrior within:
My mind will always give me more of what I focus on. Therefore, I am grateful for…

_____

_____

What do I need to hear today to keep expanding and moving forward?

_____

_____

What are 3 things I can complete to make today a success?

_____

_____

What pictures am I creating right now about that future I want?

_____

_____

The mind does not know the difference between real and imagined, so see yourself already having your desires right now and watch it become reality. Close your eyes and see, hear, touch, and feel it.

"Accept - than act. Whatever the present moment contains accept it as if you had chosen it. Always work with it, not against it... This will miraculously transform your whole life. -Eckhart Tolle

Accept is an action you do to recognize something as valid or correct, your consent to receive. Most people fight the events in their life, staying stuck in a constant war. Just ACCEPT life!

Questions to develop the Warrior within:
My mind will always give me more of what I focus on. Therefore, I am grateful for…

_____

_____

_____

What do I need to hear today to keep expanding and moving forward?

_____

_____

What are 3 things I can complete to make today a success?

_____

_____

_____

What pictures am I creating right now about that future I want?

_____

_____

_____

The mind does not know the difference between real and imagined, so see yourself already having your desires right now and watch it become reality. Close your eyes and see, hear, touch, and feel it.

"Commitment means staying loyal to what you said you were going to do long after the mood you said it in has left you. -Unknown

Commitment is a word with powerful force and magnitude. It should not be used lightly, for it holds the actions to bring all results forward. Commitment is the act of staying on course until the results are achieved. Do not make Commitments until YOU ARE READY!

Questions to develop the Warrior within:
My mind will always give me more of what I focus on. Therefore, I am grateful for...

_____

_____

_____

What do I need to hear today to keep expanding and moving forward?

_____

_____

_____

What are 3 things I can complete to make today a success?

_____

_____

_____

What pictures am I creating right now about that future I want?

_____

_____

_____

The mind does not know the difference between real and imagined, so see yourself already having your desires right now and watch it become reality. Close your eyes and see, hear, touch, and feel it.

"Great Minds discuss Ideas. Average Minds discuss Events. Small Minds discuss People. -Eleanor Roosevelt

What are you discussing in your world? What does that say about you? Remember Gossip dies when it enters the ears of the wise. Be the wise one. What others say is only a reflection of themselves, not you. Can anyone ever know the truth, only opinions of the truth, right? Notice your words.

Questions to develop the Warrior within:
My mind will always give me more of what I focus on. Therefore, I am grateful for…

_____

_____

_____

What do I need to hear today to keep expanding and moving forward?

_____

_____

_____

What are 3 things I can complete to make today a success?

_____

_____

_____

What pictures am I creating right now about that future I want?

_____

_____

_____

The mind does not know the difference between real and imagined, so see yourself already having your desires right now and watch it become reality. Close your eyes and see, hear, touch, and feel it.

"Positive self-talk is the secret whistle that calls forth your inner sleeping giant. -Michael Adams

There is a powerful unlimited giant with the strength and endurance to acquire and give you anything, once it is unleashed. It is only awakened when you cultivate your mind with mental positivity and mental muscle. Ensure you are speaking to yourself with strength, love and support.

Questions to develop the Warrior within:
My mind will always give me more of what I focus on. Therefore, I am grateful for…

_____

_____

_____

What do I need to hear today to keep expanding and moving forward?

_____

_____

What are 3 things I can complete to make today a success?

_____

_____

What pictures am I creating right now about that future I want?

_____

_____

The mind does not know the difference between real and imagined, so see yourself already having your desires right now and watch it become reality. Close your eyes and see, hear, touch, and feel it.

"Keep your thoughts positive because your thoughts become your words. Keep your words positive because your words become your behaviors. Keep your behaviors positive because your behaviors become your habits. Keep your habits positive because your habits become your values. Keep your values positive because your values become your identity. -Mahatma Ghandi

Everything in you is linked and connected!

Questions to develop the Warrior within:
My mind will always give me more of what I focus on. Therefore, I am grateful for...

_____

_____

_____

What do I need to hear today to keep expanding and moving forward?

_____

_____

What are 3 things I can complete to make today a success?

_____

_____

_____

What pictures am I creating right now about that future I want?

_____

_____

_____

The mind does not know the difference between real and imagined, so see yourself already having your desires right now and watch it become reality. Close your eyes and see, hear, touch, and feel it.

"Your reality is created by your attention. -Michael Adams

Attention is taking notice of someone or something, regarding someone or something as important or interesting. Attention is singular, meaning one event, one experience. Shifting attention can be easy, Your reality, good or bad, is simply a result of what you choose to pay attention to. What are you giving importance to?

Questions to develop the Warrior within:
My mind will always give me more of what I focus on. Therefore, I am grateful for...

_____

_____

_____

What do I need to hear today to keep expanding and moving forward?

_____

_____

_____

What are 3 things I can complete to make today a success?

_____

_____

_____

What pictures am I creating right now about that future I want?

_____

_____

_____

The mind does not know the difference between real and imagined, so see yourself already having your desires right now and watch it become reality. Close your eyes and see, hear, touch, and feel it.

"Human beings absolutely follow through on who they believe they are. -Tony Robbins

Never underestimate the power of your beliefs. Your beliefs are exactly at this moment attuned to your current behaviors. Therefore, your follow through is in alignment with what you think you are able to have and not have. Question your beliefs and change yourself. Ask yourself for what purpose do I hold this belief?

Questions to develop the Warrior within:
My mind will always give me more of what I focus on. Therefore, I am grateful for...

_____

_____

_____

What do I need to hear today to keep expanding and moving forward?

_____

_____

_____

What are 3 things I can complete to make today a success?

_____

_____

_____

What pictures am I creating right now about that future I want?

_____

_____

_____

The mind does not know the difference between real and imagined, so see yourself already having your desires right now and watch it become reality. Close your eyes and see, hear, touch, and feel it.

"Actions prove who someone is, words just prove who they want to be. -Unknown

Are you backing up your words with action? To back up your words means to take the type of action that creates discomfort, fear, and embarrassment. Those are the types of actions that must be taken by you. The rewards are priceless and in the direction of your dream life.

Questions to develop the Warrior within:
My mind will always give me more of what I focus on. Therefore, I am grateful for...

_____

_____

_____

What do I need to hear today to keep expanding and moving forward?

_____

_____

What are 3 things I can complete to make today a success?

_____

_____

_____

What pictures am I creating right now about that future I want?

_____

_____

_____

The mind does not know the difference between real and imagined, so see yourself already having your desires right now and watch it become reality. Close your eyes and see, hear, touch, and feel it.

"A negative mind will never give you a positive life. - Unknown

The only time more negatives will give you a positive is in math. Any other time, a negative mind will only breed and fester more negativity, doubt, failure, stress, anger, criticism, hate. What do you think a positive mind will create? Will you be willing to develop the positivity required to have that life?

Questions to develop the Warrior within:
My mind will always give me more of what I focus on. Therefore, I am grateful for...

_____

_____

_____

What do I need to hear today to keep expanding and moving forward?

_____

_____

_____

What are 3 things I can complete to make today a success?

_____

_____

_____

What pictures am I creating right now about that future I want?

_____

_____

_____

The mind does not know the difference between real and imagined, so see yourself already having your desires right now and watch it become reality. Close your eyes and see, hear, touch, and feel it.

"Success is never owned, it's rented and the rent is due everyday. -Rory Vaden

Take the example of your physical body. If you have a body you love to show others, it is a guarantee you pay the rent daily to keep that body. You make choices in food that allow you to keep that physique. You put in the sweat to maintain the muscle. Now, how can this be transferred to other areas of life?

Questions to develop the Warrior within:
My mind will always give me more of what I focus on. Therefore, I am grateful for…

_____

_____

_____

What do I need to hear today to keep expanding and moving forward?

_____

_____

_____

What are 3 things I can complete to make today a success?

_____

_____

_____

What pictures am I creating right now about that future I want?

_____

_____

_____

The mind does not know the difference between real and imagined, so see yourself already having your desires right now and watch it become reality. Close your eyes and see, hear, touch, and feel it.

"There is no elevator to success you have to take the stairs. -Zig Ziglar

Your success is atop the staircase, you must take every step required. No matter how much your legs burn and body aches, your success will remain in its place. Every step taken is necessary. Do you dare to keep stepping? If it's hard, do it hard. Embrace the challenge, know it is part of the journey.

Questions to develop the Warrior within:
My mind will always give me more of what I focus on. Therefore, I am grateful for...

_____

_____

_____

What do I need to hear today to keep expanding and moving forward?

_____

_____

What are 3 things I can complete to make today a success?

_____

_____

What pictures am I creating right now about that future I want?

_____

_____

The mind does not know the difference between real and imagined, so see yourself already having your desires right now and watch it become reality. Close your eyes and see, hear, touch, and feel it.

"Some people dream of success while others wake up and work hard at it. -Napolean Hill

Are you dreaming or working hard? At some point, dreams must be followed through with action to bring them down from the clouds and into reality. A plan is your bridge that links you from where you are now to where your dream is. Hard work and action are the steps you take to cross the bridge.

Questions to develop the Warrior within:
My mind will always give me more of what I focus on. Therefore, I am grateful for…

_____

_____

_____

What do I need to hear today to keep expanding and moving forward?

_____

_____

_____

What are 3 things I can complete to make today a success?

_____

_____

_____

What pictures am I creating right now about that future I want?

_____

_____

_____

The mind does not know the difference between real and imagined, so see yourself already having your desires right now and watch it become reality. Close your eyes and see, hear, touch, and feel it.

"I have learned over the years that when one's mind is made up, that diminishes fear, knowing what must be done does away with fear. -Rosa Parks

Is your mind made up on what you want in life? Do you know what must be done to get it? Having this much certainty can almost eliminate fear completely. Make up your mind, so that your mind can get you what you most desire.

Questions to develop the Warrior within:
My mind will always give me more of what I focus on. Therefore, I am grateful for...

_____

_____

_____

What do I need to hear today to keep expanding and moving forward?

_____

_____

_____

What are 3 things I can complete to make today a success?

_____

_____

_____

What pictures am I creating right now about that future I want?

_____

_____

_____

The mind does not know the difference between real and imagined, so see yourself already having your desires right now and watch it become reality. Close your eyes and see, hear, touch, and feel it.

"Grow through, what you go through. –Unknown

Think of all your obstacles as growing moments. A plant has no other choice, but to keep growing. No matter what the weather conditions around it are, the plant grows through what it goes through. We must do the same and grow from the experiences we go through in life no matter what type of conditions. We have the built in mechanics to do it.

Questions to develop the Warrior within:
My mind will always give me more of what I focus on. Therefore, I am grateful for...

_____

_____

_____

What do I need to hear today to keep expanding and moving forward?

_____

_____

What are 3 things I can complete to make today a success?

_____

_____

_____

What pictures am I creating right now about that future I want?

_____

_____

_____

The mind does not know the difference between real and imagined, so see yourself already having your desires right now and watch it become reality. Close your eyes and see, hear, touch, and feel it.

"Vocabulary enables us to interpret and express. If you have a limited vocabulary, you will also have a limited vision and a limited future. -Jim Rohn

Vocabulary is the body of words known to an individual person. The grandness of your future will always be dictated by the amount of words you can use to express what you want. Expand your vocabulary to expand your future.

Questions to develop the Warrior within:
My mind will always give me more of what I focus on. Therefore, I am grateful for…

_____

_____

_____

What do I need to hear today to keep expanding and moving forward?

_____

_____

_____

What are 3 things I can complete to make today a success?

_____

_____

_____

What pictures am I creating right now about that future I want?

_____

_____

_____

The mind does not know the difference between real and imagined, so see yourself already having your desires right now and watch it become reality. Close your eyes and see, hear, touch, and feel it.

"When our hearts turn to our ancestors, something changes inside us. We feel part of something greater than ourselves. -Russell M. Nelson

YOU are always a walking product of those who came before you. You represent greatness every time you wake up, a certain genius that exists within you. Knowing that you are connected to ancient wisdom, you are never alone. Acknowledge and feel that connection right now."

Questions to develop the Warrior within:
My mind will always give me more of what I focus on. Therefore, I am grateful for...

_____

_____

What do I need to hear today to keep expanding and moving forward?

_____

_____

What are 3 things I can complete to make today a success?

_____

_____

What pictures am I creating right now about that future I want?

_____

_____

The mind does not know the difference between real and imagined, so see yourself already having your desires right now and watch it become reality. Close your eyes and see, hear, touch, and feel it.

"A lesson is repeated until learned. A lesson will be presented to you in various forms until you have learned it. Once you have learned it, you can move on to the next lesson. -Cherie Carter-Scott

This is a life rule, so next time you find yourself in a similar position, don't ask why? Ask what do I need to learn? Life has essential lessons that are essential to you learning before you proceed forward. What has repeated itself in your life?

Questions to develop the Warrior within:
My mind will always give me more of what I focus on. Therefore, I am grateful for…

_____

_____

_____

What do I need to hear today to keep expanding and moving forward?

_____

_____

_____

What are 3 things I can complete to make today a success?

_____

_____

_____

What pictures am I creating right now about that future I want?

_____

_____

_____

The mind does not know the difference between real and imagined, so see yourself already having your desires right now and watch it become reality. Close your eyes and see, hear, touch, and feel it.

"Go within everyday and find the inner strength so that the world will not blow your candle out. - Katherine Dunham

Going in means to meditate daily. Meditate is to think deeply or focus one's mind for a period of time, in silence for spiritual or relaxation purpose. The inside is not empty, but full of answers when you can silence the voice inside. Make use of this power.

Questions to develop the Warrior within:
My mind will always give me more of what I focus on. Therefore, I am grateful for...

_____

_____

_____

What do I need to hear today to keep expanding and moving forward?

_____

_____

_____

What are 3 things I can complete to make today a success?

_____

_____

_____

What pictures am I creating right now about that future I want?

_____

_____

_____

The mind does not know the difference between real and imagined, so see yourself already having your desires right now and watch it become reality. Close your eyes and see, hear, touch, and feel it.

"If we are not a little bit uncomfortable every day, we're not growing. All the good stuff is outside our comfort zone. -Jack Canfield

Would you like to be a little uncomfortable today or tomorrow? Why? Remember we cannot shrink into our dreams and goals. We need to expand into them. Expanding means growing, discomfort, unease, but ALL WORTH IT! Trust me, YOUR Future self will thank you with for stepping up.

Questions to develop the Warrior within:
My mind will always give me more of what I focus on. Therefore, I am grateful for...

_____

_____

_____

What do I need to hear today to keep expanding and moving forward?

_____

_____

_____

What are 3 things I can complete to make today a success?

_____

_____

_____

What pictures am I creating right now about that future I want?

_____

_____

_____

The mind does not know the difference between real and imagined, so see yourself already having your desires right now and watch it become reality. Close your eyes and see, hear, touch, and feel it.

"Perpetual optimism is a force multiplier. -Colin Powell

Continually being optimistic about how you see the world will multiply the amount of opportunities and experiences available to you. One thousand doors, one thousand possibilities. Never underestimate your choice on how you see something. There are always thousands of angles in which to see something.

Questions to develop the Warrior within:

My mind will always give me more of what I focus on. Therefore, I am grateful for…

_____

_____

_____

What do I need to hear today to keep expanding and moving forward?

_____

_____

What are 3 things I can complete to make today a success?

_____

_____

_____

What pictures am I creating right now about that future I want?

_____

_____

_____

The mind does not know the difference between real and imagined, so see yourself already having your desires right now and watch it become reality. Close your eyes and see, hear, touch, and feel it.

**"Your energy introduces you before you even speak. -
Unknown**

**Whether you know it or not, your energy can be felt by
others. Just like when you can feel someone is not
themselves. Monitor the energy you put out, your
words can't hide what others can see. How will you
want your energy to introduce you? Full of life, love,
excitement? Or an energy drain?**

Questions to develop the Warrior within:
My mind will always give me more of what I focus on. Therefore, I am
grateful for...

_____

_____

_____

What do I need to hear today to keep expanding and moving forward?

_____

_____

What are 3 things I can complete to make today a success?

_____

_____

What pictures am I creating right now about that future I want?

_____

_____

The mind does not know the difference between real and imagined, so see
yourself already having your desires right now and watch it become
reality. Close your eyes and see, hear, touch, and feel it.

"Before you make any decision, consider its effect on the next seven generations. -Hopi Proverb

How we live today by the choices and decisions we make will impact those that will come after us. Future children, grandchildren, great grandchildren. How do you want to be remembered in the long lineage you will be creating? Our responsibility for life extends beyond our lifetime.

Questions to develop the Warrior within:
My mind will always give me more of what I focus on. Therefore, I am grateful for...

_____

_____

_____

What do I need to hear today to keep expanding and moving forward?

_____

_____

What are 3 things I can complete to make today a success?

_____

_____

What pictures am I creating right now about that future I want?

_____

_____

The mind does not know the difference between real and imagined, so see yourself already having your desires right now and watch it become reality. Close your eyes and see, hear, touch, and feel it.

"A relationship with no trust is like a phone with no service. And what do you do with a phone with no service? You play games. -Unknown

Trust is backing up your words with actions. You can only control your choices and behaviors. If you have lost trust, know that there will be nothing good without it restored. Admit your mistakes now, save yourself the grief.

Questions to develop the Warrior within:
My mind will always give me more of what I focus on. Therefore, I am grateful for...

_____

_____

_____

What do I need to hear today to keep expanding and moving forward?

_____

_____

_____

What are 3 things I can complete to make today a success?

_____

_____

_____

What pictures am I creating right now about that future I want?

_____

_____

_____

The mind does not know the difference between real and imagined, so see yourself already having your desires right now and watch it become reality. Close your eyes and see, hear, touch, and feel it.

"I am always doing that which I cannot do today, in order that I may learn how to do it. -Pablo Picasso

Learning always takes this progression. You start with something you know nothing about or cannot do at all, then you jump in and try to do it. You make mistakes. You gain feedback about what not to do next time. You continue with practice. Then you LEARN IT. Then it becomes AUTOMATIC.

Questions to develop the Warrior within:
My mind will always give me more of what I focus on. Therefore, I am grateful for...

_____

_____

_____

What do I need to hear today to keep expanding and moving forward?

_____

_____

_____

What are 3 things I can complete to make today a success?

_____

_____

_____

What pictures am I creating right now about that future I want?

_____

_____

_____

The mind does not know the difference between real and imagined, so see yourself already having your desires right now and watch it become reality. Close your eyes and see, hear, touch, and feel it.

"If egg is broken by outside force, life ends. If broken by inside force, life begins. Great things always begin from inside. -Jim Kwik

This is a powerful truth. If you are not strong inside, the forces from outside can end it. However, when you become strong from the inside and can break through your own shell, an extraordinary being is revealed. Always seek to build your inner strength.

Questions to develop the Warrior within:
My mind will always give me more of what I focus on. Therefore, I am grateful for…

_____

_____

_____

What do I need to hear today to keep expanding and moving forward?

_____

_____

_____

What are 3 things I can complete to make today a success?

_____

_____

_____

What pictures am I creating right now about that future I want?

_____

_____

_____

The mind does not know the difference between real and imagined, so see yourself already having your desires right now and watch it become reality. Close your eyes and see, hear, touch, and feel it.

"Conviction is a force multiplier. If you want something claim it in your gut. The universe itself responds to your inner certainty. -Marianne Williamson

The forces of the universe will multiply and align when you are so certain and convinced about getting something. Conviction, to be convinced of or firmly hold a belief. This is the type of feeling you want when pursuing your dreams.

Questions to develop the Warrior within:
My mind will always give me more of what I focus on. Therefore, I am grateful for...

_____

_____

_____

What do I need to hear today to keep expanding and moving forward?

_____

_____

_____

What are 3 things I can complete to make today a success?

_____

_____

_____

What pictures am I creating right now about that future I want?

_____

_____

_____

The mind does not know the difference between real and imagined, so see yourself already having your desires right now and watch it become reality. Close your eyes and see, hear, touch, and feel it.

"Action is the real measure of INTELLIGENCE. - Napolean Hill

An ordinary person becomes an extraordinary person along the road of action. Everyone who you think is smarter than you, better than you, richer than you, braver than you, happier than you, more positive than you, have all taken MORE ACTION THAN YOU! You become what you do!

Questions to develop the Warrior within:
My mind will always give me more of what I focus on. Therefore, I am grateful for...

_____

_____

_____

What do I need to hear today to keep expanding and moving forward?

_____

_____

_____

What are 3 things I can complete to make today a success?

_____

_____

_____

What pictures am I creating right now about that future I want?

_____

_____

_____

The mind does not know the difference between real and imagined, so see yourself already having your desires right now and watch it become reality. Close your eyes and see, hear, touch, and feel it.

"The man who has no imagination has no wings. - Muhammad Ali

Where can your imagination take you? We often discredit the imagination as a childish act, like pretend play. However, the imagination holds the power to create, to heal, to visualize, to experience, and to have. It is your greatest tool you were born with. Make sure you use it to become your greatness!

Questions to develop the Warrior within:
My mind will always give me more of what I focus on. Therefore, I am grateful for…

_____

_____

_____

What do I need to hear today to keep expanding and moving forward?

_____

_____

_____

What are 3 things I can complete to make today a success?

_____

_____

_____

What pictures am I creating right now about that future I want?

_____

_____

_____

The mind does not know the difference between real and imagined, so see yourself already having your desires right now and watch it become reality. Close your eyes and see, hear, touch, and feel it.

"Here's to the crazy ones, the misfits, the rebels, the troublemakers, the round pegs in the square holes, the ones who see things differently. They're not fond of rules. You can quote them, disagree with them, glorify or vilify them, but the only thing you can't do is ignore them because they change things? The ones who are crazy enough to think that they can change the world, are the ones who do. -Steve Jobs

When you don't out of place, the warrior is speaking.

Questions to develop the Warrior within:
My mind will always give me more of what I focus on. Therefore, I am grateful for...

_____

_____

_____

What do I need to hear today to keep expanding and moving forward?

_____

_____

What are 3 things I can complete to make today a success?

_____

_____

_____

What pictures am I creating right now about that future I want?

_____

_____

_____

The mind does not know the difference between real and imagined, so see yourself already having your desires right now and watch it become reality. Close your eyes and see, hear, touch, and feel it.

"As children of a diverse culture, we must understand that we carry forth value and benefit in our ways. Never feel less than. Be grateful to those who gifted us with the honor of carrying it forward. -Michael Adams

Every single youth was brought into this world at the exact time and place they were meant to. You are all equipped with the right ingredients to move the people forward with respect and honor.

Questions to develop the Warrior within:
My mind will always give me more of what I focus on. Therefore, I am grateful for…

_____

_____

_____

What do I need to hear today to keep expanding and moving forward?

_____

_____

_____

What are 3 things I can complete to make today a success?

_____

_____

_____

What pictures am I creating right now about that future I want?

_____

_____

_____

The mind does not know the difference between real and imagined, so see yourself already having your desires right now and watch it become reality. Close your eyes and see, hear, touch, and feel it.

Congratulations Warrior!

You have completed this book which means you are in the top 10% of people who actually complete what they start. Most people start books, but simply never finish. Imagine over time, what that does to our TRUST in ourselves in our own ability to complete something or do what we say. I promise you, if you simply start completing more things in your life, little by little you are restoring your inner TRUST in your word which has the power to completely transform your life.

Did you know that the word CONFIDENCE actually has strong relations to the word TRUST? Yes the degree of confidence you have is directly proportionate to the degree of trust you have in yourself. The latin root of confidence is confidere, deep trust. What if you had absolute trust in yourself that everything would be fine every time you walked into a new situation? The need for confidence would not even be needed, right? So trust that you are exactly where you need to be right now in your life. This book came across your path for a reason. Now, let your journey continue.

The fact that you completed this book means that you are ready to allow that bigger vision of yourself come through. That inner warrior is ready to be developed. This book is a first step towards you creating more in your life and to help you on your journey, I have some free trainings to assist.

Free Training #1: Hypnotic Confidence Audio - this 24 minute audio is designed to create all the confidence you'll ever need. Truth is, most people try to make changes with confidence through their conscious effort and wonder why nothing ever changes. However, the most powerful place to work from is at the subconscious level, which contains our values, beliefs, and identity. Hypnosis is a technique used to make those shifts subconsciously, so you can get the results you desire.
https://www.nextwavewarrior.com/pl/42641

Free Training #2: Vertical Thought Formula - this 80 minute audio training is designed to teach you how to use your mind and thinking ability to get you what you want and eliminate what you don't want in your life. Most people stay stuck in their problems because they were never taught how to eliminate them. I guarantee that you have the tools to eliminate any problem, stress, anger, frustration, etc. This super valuable training will teach you just how you can erase any problem using your ability to think. https://www.nextwavewarrior.com/pl/44748

Join me for more development at www.nextwavewarrior.com

Made in the USA
Middletown, DE
01 May 2022

65090995R00060